G Up Again

An amazing story about a family that became homeless and use it to raise awareness about the homelessless of others,

Shonta Gibson & Eddie Bell

TABLE OF CONTENTS

Dedication 1

Chapter 1: The Voice 2

Chapter 2: I Don't Want To Leave But I Got To Go Right Now 6

Chapter 3: Foster Family 10

Chapter 4 Weekly Busness 13

Chapter 5 Tunnel Life 15

Chapter 6 Create A Lane 27

Chapter 7 Finally Home 34

Chapter 8 The Approval 36

Chapter 9 Four Heartbeats 40

Chapter 10 Awareness 45

Community Resources: Las Vagas 49-51

Queen G Live Exprence 52

LGEN Film 53

Dedication

I would like to thank God for shining his grace, favor, and mercy upon my families life. To my parents Tyrone Gibson Sr. and Pricilla Murray, thank you for creating me. To my siblings Salendra Durham, Tyrone Gibson Jr. ,Tyrese Gibson, Nyesha Gibson, and Savon Gibson, I love you. To my 7 heartbeats, Tanisha Chambers, Star Rolle, Madison Green, Eric Green, Heaven Gibson Bell, Serenity Gibson Bell, Divinity, Gibson Bell, I love you with everything in me. Im so grateful that God chose you to be my beautiful seeds. To my three grand heartbeats Alayah Davis, Isiah Davis, and September Rolle, granny loves you. To my loving husband Eddie Bell, we have weathered so many storms together going on 12 years now. Im so grateful that God chose you to stand by my side in life, and that he spared your life for 40 years on this earth. You are now able to see the fruits of your labor and witness God's continued greatness in your life and through your gifted hands. Your life is a true testimony. To The Foster family that took my family in for two weeks thank you. To Michelle Hooker, I will never forget the sacrifice that you made on behalf of my family in our homeless crisis, thank you. Thank you Juliet Owens for being there for my family and birthing a brilliant man into the world. Thank you Billy and Vaneta Easter of Assistance of Southern Nevada. Thank you Justin Roberts, and Javon Jackson of True Family Services for supporting my family. To Kenneth and Melody Dorsey of Planet Mike Earth, thank you for your support of Operation Bring Your Best. To Shawn Borland of Unique 702 Clothing, thank you for supporting our movement. To all who donated their time and money to Operation Bring Your best, and all that were there for us in our crisis, your seed will never be forgotten. Special thanks to Andrew Bennet who stood by our side through thick and thin as we built Operation Bring Your Best. To Arthur Mcclen and Teresa Mcclenaghan of Holy Smoke Misfit Missionaries, thank you for showing us that the homeless crisis exists under the grounds of Las Vegas. Thank you Dj Thump, Dj Remix, Vegas Urban Pride, Minister Stretch, and Trina Jiles for your support of Operation Bring Your Best. If you bought us groceries, allowed us to crash at your home, or transported my family during our homeless crisis, thank you. To all the unspoken heroes who take care of the community and less fortunate, I thank you all from the bottom of my heart.

Chapter 1
The Voice

May of 2016, I lived in Las Vegas with my family. Me, my husband Eddie Bell, and our four children were all in a good space, enjoying life. We had a home with three bedrooms, food on the table, hubby was working, had two cars, and the kids were all doing well in school. If there were something called perfect life, that's what we were living "Our Best Life." We were in the money zone and everything. Nothing could stop us from enjoying life. As you know life is life, and it has a way of throwing curveballs that you least expect. One weekend in May, I had to head to California to do hair. Amazingly Ca. and Vegas is only 4 hours away, so I could take regular work trips without skipping a beat. Anyway, my Husband, Eddie walked me to the car, and said a traveling prayer with me like always, and would stand out to watch the car hit the end of the block before he returned into the house. I had a total of 5 hair clients that weekend, so once I went up the highway, it was all work no play. On those types of intense work trips, I would drive to my client's home, service them, then head to the next. I had to stay focused and get these clients knocked out. Getting tired was never an option. I successfully finished all five of my clients that weekend and crashed and burned. My body gave out on me. I crashed at a client because I was so tired. I was awakened out of my sleep, with a voice. That Voice said, "Get Up." The voice that I heard was kind enough but stern enough to understand that this was coming from a spiritual place that was deep, and it was important for me to listen. It was around 6 am, and although groggy and tired, I followed " The Voice." That was the longest 4-hour journey of my life. I tried drinking coke, playing loud music, and talking to myself. I did whatever it took to stay awake. When I arrived in Las Vegas, I was so happy. The last couple of miles dragged out, and my last twenty minutes felt like 4 hours all over again. I finally made it home, and like always, happy to see my family when I come off of one of those work trips. When I hit the door, all 4 kids ran up to me yelling "Mommy, Mommy." I kissed my husband like how I always do. Everything was on track so far. I asked my honey if he could go and run errands for me because I was too tired. Now keep in mind it's the middle of summer in Las Vegas, and if anybody knows about Las Vegas summers, it feels like what I can only imagine hell feels like. Luckily we had a.c. in the car. He agreed to go run errands for me. I'm so grateful for a husband that is a team with me, and that doesn't complain much. While he ran errands, I prepared dinner early because I knew that especially that night I would crash from being so exhausted. My kids were always so excited to eat mommy's cooking. Hubby gets back from the errands and immediately comes in peeling clothes off because it was so hot outside. He was stripped of his shirt and just had on some shorts. He ended up going to the backyard to smoke a cigarette and came to sit down in the chair that was in the middle of the kitchen. Well, I noticed that he plopped down, almost losing all extremities and the use of his own body. I was like hold up wait, this is turning into something else. I ran over to him to hold him up and immediately got on the phone with 911. He was trying to tell me that he loved me while slurring his words. He sounded like someone that had been to the dentist. I had never seen someone have a stroke before but my young 36-year-old husband was experiencing a stroke. Omg, I was so scared but trying to be strong for him. I'm holding him up in the chair, keeping the kids out of the kitchen, while talking to 911. I was trying everything to hold the tears back. I had to be strong for my family at that moment. The ambulance got there within 7 minutes and was able to visually see that his face was slurring on one side, which meant he was having a stroke. They didn't waste any time, they went right into action checking vitals, and seeing if he was alert. I couldn't join him in the ambulance due to the kids being there. I would join him later on at UMC hospital one of our local community hospitals. The up and coming days after his stroke were hard. Besides the physical changes to his face and speech, there were also memory changes. I noticed immediately that he couldn't retain much information and his responses to things were slower. You never know with strokes if the recovery is going to be short or long. The bravest thing that I saw Eddie do was go live on Facebook two days after his stroke, while hooked up to all the I .v.s. He pleaded to his audience, that having a stroke is not about age, that it can happen to anyone. At this age of 36, it was shocking to everyone that it happened to him as a young man. The doctors were in awe of that as well. He got really high views on that life because everyone was shocked. It was so hard for me to see him hooked to all of those I.V.s and machines. Most times when I went to go see him, he was medicated. I had to be strong for him and the kids. He got on the phone and called his mom crying, explaining to her that he needs her by his side because he almost died. In all these years that I've been with him, I had never seen a teardrop come from his face at all, so I knew this was serious. With the urgency in his voice and the tears in his eyes, it made me cry. She heard the urgency in his voice and was there the next day, on the next flight. Mom ended up being with us an entire week for support. It was perfect because I and she traded off equally between the kids and visiting him in the hospital. You don't realize how much a person is valued until they are not 100 percent healthy.

Chapter 2
I Don't Want To Leave But I Gotta Go Right Now

My days following his stroke were hard considering I had to hold the whole family down. I had to adjust to a new lifestyle quickly with Eddie recovering from his stroke. The doctor advised him not to drive, or be in stressful environments. His memory was also affected by the stroke, so I found myself repeating things to him over and over. I could tell that the stroke hit him hard because normally his memory was sharp. Everything was keen like his sense of direction down to remembering a grocery list before, after the stroke I had to write things down for him or repeat things regularly. I was really frustrated but couldn't add stress to him at all. I kept the mood in the house very mellow and somber, not triggering him in any way. Let us talk about the financial responsibility that was thrown in my lap. He couldn't return to work right away, so I had to find money that didn't exist. Robbing Peter to pay Paul was an understatement. This is when I learned that I had to ask people for help. We were the ones that were normally in a position to give to others, and now we were in need. Sometimes $35 was enough to keep our lights on, and sometimes we borrowed money that was hard to give back, but because we needed it we had to ask people. The largest amount that we had to borrow was $400 that would help us pay our rent. I started running out of people to hit up. Doors started closing in our face, and most times you couldn't come back the same way. I was the type that felt bad that we needed help. For the sake of my babies, I had to do what I needed to do. People began to look at us like " What's wrong with you." "Why can't you get it together?" It took everything in me not to break down and give up. We were receiving food stamps at the time and would have to let people use them so that we could get cash to pay for utilities. I hated to get up every day. We went from a perfect two-year rental history to having to pay major late fees to keep us from being evicted. This is when I learned the game that property companies play. Robbing from people like us and taking advantage of someone that's down. The late fees would be 300 plus dollars a month on top of our 1100 monthly rent. We were beginning to lose all the way around. I started realizing that we might not be able to save this situation. This was starting to take over and overwhelm my family. I was frustrated because normally I could come up with a plan or a solution, but I was losing. There were days that I just didn't know anymore. I had a realistic talk with my husband. " Do you think we should just get storage and be done with this?" He replied, "Let's try to fight for it." "Ok babe, but we are running out of resources and people to reach out to." The upcoming days were so hard, not even knowing if we would even be able to keep our lights on. In June of 2016, I reached out to family again for the help, and by then they were tired. My brother surprisingly looked out for my family and blessed me with $1600.00 to pay the rent. The office was shocked when we brought a cashier's check in there for that amount. The rental property was rooting for us so bringing that in there made them happy. We were in the safe zone for one month, but I already started thinking about July. I couldn't help but try to figure something out in advance. Well, July hit and rent was already due. I came to my husband again and made a plea that we need to let go. There was no way that we could keep going like this. We realistically weighed our options and sought after cheap storage. We had no ultimate plan but we just started packing. The home was 3 bedrooms, two baths, so we had a lot of houses to pack. We started with the most important to the least important in that order. What was high on the priority list was getting our paperwork together, and then sorting through the kid's clothes. Some things that we just didn't need we either gave it away or tossed it. We started receiving notices around the 10th of July from the office. It was a warning to pay or quit. We were already packed so I just placed the notices in the stack with the rest of the shut-off notices, or threats. You have to really reach to a deep place within not let anything bother you. My main focus was to get as many belongings out as soon as possible. At the same time, I was cleaning and packing. We accumulated so much stuff in that little amount of time that we were there. The kids were curious about why we were moving. Kids didn't understand that we were are about to lose our place. I just explained to them that we were going to pick a new house. On the 28th of July, I woke up with the big Eviction notice on the gate. It was huge and taped to the outside of my gate. I felt so embarrassed because in my entire adult life of renting apartments, and homes, I never ever got one of these. It basically stated that we had 24 hours to vacate the property. Due to the fact that we got a head start, it wasn't as bad, but it was still bad. It was all bad because on the other end of this notice we had nowhere to go. That was the scary part. Well while packing, I went to social media. I didn't talk about what happened or anything but it was something in my live video that alerted one of my good friends to reach out to me. She called me right away after seeing that life on Facebook. Her name is Deb, she asked me, "What's Wrong?" " I got an eviction today, and I have to be out in 24 hours. I'm heartbroken and don't know where to take my family. We have no plan and this has never happened before." "Well don't stress out, when you get the rest of your things out just come here. We don't know where this is going to go, but I do have a guest bedroom that your family can stay in. Whatever you do don't stress." As tears rolled down my face from gratefulness, I thanked her and went immediately to let my husband know the good news. He said, "God is good all the time." Amen

Chapter 3
FOSTER FAMILY

The chapter closed on being in our home, and thankfully we had a landing spot. We went from our 3 bedroom two bathroom house, into our friend's place which had a guest room for the 6 of us. It was Deb, Elle her husband, and they had 6 foster children. When we added our family to their home it ended up being a total of 4 adults and 10 kids under one roof. It was a major adjustment to move from our own space to come into a space that's not yours. I reminded the kids constantly that it wasn't our place and they needed to be good. It was so much pressure to go from the kids having their own space of a whole house to us being confined to one room, that had not.v. All 6 of us stayed in the guest room of the home because all of the other rooms of the home were occupied with children from their families. I tried not to come out of the room that often just to give the fam space. It was a very difficult time for me, especially still not having a plan. I felt very depressed all the time. I still did my entertainment blogs, but they were based on what I was going through. They were usually based around strength, pain, getting through life with prayer and not giving up on family. People really started tuning in closer, but the torture was that I couldn't reveal what was going on. I was very transparent with my viewing audience but had to keep this part private. It took everything in me to not give up considering I felt like a failure. I was living a double life. I was an entertainer that lost it all. Deb wouldn't accept money from us so we just bought food for the home with the food stamps that we received from the state. I just couldn't imagine laying in someone's home, pulling from their resources and not contributing. Anyways we ended up staying there for two weeks, then was called into the living room for a talk with my friends, who were also foster parents. They basically informed us in a loving way that we had to leave due to their upcoming license recertification. I was shattered in a million pieces from the news but respected their decision. We basically had no choice. That weekend I was scheduled to go to California to do hair, so my personal plans now changed into us packing the entire family up to head to Cali. I washed up all of our dirty clothes, then we packed and hit the road. I didn't even get a mile out of Las Vegas before tears starting flooding my eyes. The tears kept pouring out of me like a well. The true reality that we are officially homeless hit me and I was so emotional. I kept apologizing to my husband for breaking down. He offered comfort during that time but nothing helped. "Baby what are we going to do?" "I don't know but try to make that change from hair, and we have gone figure something out okay." "Okay honey, I'm gone try to focus on hair, that away I will earn some gas money and have enough money for food." We now have no refrigerator or stove, so we had to eat out every meal, and for a family of 6, that was expensive. We ate at Mcdonalds or would buy a box of chicken to get by. I dropped my family off at my mom's house for that weekend so that they could have a good solid meal, shower, and wash the dirty clothes that they had while I go work. My body was in the chair, and my hands were moving but my heart was with, my family. I felt like the wind was knocked out of me. We went from having a base and foundation to figuring out each step one at a time. I made enough that weekend to drive back to Vegas and afford a hotel stay for two days only. Remember I was funding meals, gas, and hotel. My money ran out after two days. I prayed so hard but felt like my prayers weren't getting through. My husband's hands were tied, and the kids were just confused. We didn't know where our next meals were coming from or what was going to happen from one minute to the next.

Chapter 4
Weekly Business

As we were trying to figure out our next moves, a friend of ours told us about weekly in Las Vegas. A weekly is a hotel room set up that rents out to people and you pay your rent week to week. Another name for this set up is an extended stay. At this point, we didn't have a lot of options, so we started looking into some weekly around town. There were a lot of these places on Boulder Hwy in Las Vegas. Just like when you search for a place to stay, we researched these the same way. We had to shop around for prices because some were higher than the others. Anyway, we walk into this one on Boulder highway and give them my name. When they ran my personal name, it showed that my rental history had been scarred from the eviction. Not only was it dinged with the main eviction, but it also showed the history of the lates, and it showed that the city of Las Vegas Placed 8 evictions on my record from the same address. I'm not sure if that's even legal, but that's how Las Vegas rental companies do you. They have you so messed up in their system, you can't rent anywhere. Anyway, they gave me a printout, and I walked out of there feeling worse. I was already down, this pushed me down even more. Our next attempt was to completely take me out of the equation and now go with my husband's name. We went to a weekly called Siegal Suites. He went to sign up, omg we got in. It was the best news that I received in a while. We got in paid the deposit and rent for that week, then we started working on the next week's rent. Whenever you're in a situation like that, the time rolls around fast. Our next step was to check the babies in the local school nearby. We got that done and got my son's transportation set up for his school. My son has cerebral palsy and required door to door pickups so wherever we live, he was always assigned transportation. Stress levels were already high, we were behind on tags, upside down on our car note, and having trouble coming up with our weekly rent. I felt financially destroyed, and just down from not knowing what I was going to do from one moment to the next. To add injury to insult, my husband went to go and take the kids to school to discover the car was gone. The finance company picked it up due to us being behind on notes. I told my husband, "Well the kids won't be able to go to school today." It was October month in Vegas and cold. Another thing, the school was 10 minutes away in driving distance but the walking distance was 30 minutes walking. Now 30 minutes wasn't so bad for just an adult walking but were talking about three little babies that were 6, and the twins were 5. After we lost our car, my husband got up every day walked them to school during the winter months to make sure that they got to school every day. Some days he got creative and would make the girls sing The song "This girl is on Fire song by Alicia Keys," just to make the time go by fast. It took my husband a total of an hour to take them and come back home then the same when the time for them to get out. I was doing a live talk show at the time called,"Morning Tea With The Queens." I had to go live every morning on this talk show platform and not show the emotion of what was really happening in my personal life. One of my co-hosts lived on the same street as me, so she would pick me up for my show every day. While he's walking them to school, I'm riding in the car on the way to set with the drama going on in the car. A lot of days my co-host had arguments with her dude on the way to set. The arguments got hostile and would almost turn violent. It was so draining with life and my trip to work. Walking on the set would be my way to have some type of relief from all of that. When you're riding with someone you can't complain about what they're going through. I damn sure wasn't going to get in their business. My life was crazy enough already.

Chapter 5
Tunnel Life

We were barely getting by in the weekly, but we did everything that we had to do to keep it because this now became the roof over our heads, so that we wouldn't be directly on the streets. One day I met Arthur McAllen and his beautiful wife Teresa while on the set of" Morning Tea With The Queens." I was so impressed with their mission called Holy Smoke Misfit Missionaries. This nonprofit was created to go out to smoke and put a smile on the faces of the homeless through comedy. They also provided food and clothing. The amazing part is that they served the people in a secret area under the grounds of Las Vegas. I had no idea that the homeless lived in the drainage system of Las Vegas.

During our show that day I promised them that one day I would join their mission and bring more awareness to what they were doing. In January of 2017, I finally got to join them. They picked me up one Tuesday night from the weekly to join their mission. I didn't know what to expect really. Honestly, I was a bit nervous the first time. Although we were displaced from our home we had a roof at that moment. These people actually lived outside. It was cold that evening so I bundled up and took a walk. I'm not gone tell you exactly where we went to check on the homeless. I will say that when I looked up there were casinos such as beautiful Mandalay Bay amongst other hotels. I was really shocked to discover that such a harsh way of life existed right under these beautiful casinos in Las Vegas that people visit all year. The people were hidden under the tunnels. We went to whats called a camp, which is a base where the

homeless set up their tents and makeshift homes. The first thing that I noticed was the terrible smell that reeked of feces, alcohol, and other things. The first camp that we hit drew me to tears because the home of one of the guys was a box literally. On the other side of that box, you could see his alcohol bottles from him drinking himself away. This gentleman was very depressed and he expressed it with his drinking. The sight of this base was so sad. I made the decision that night that I was going to use my media platform to bring awareness to this way of life. I remember walking away from that mission feeling disgusted and frustrated. We filmed that night and my reactions to tears and disbelief were genuine. I was so numb. One of my first thoughts was to have my husband film so that we bring awareness by creating documentaries. I went consecutively as often as I could, joining Holy Smoke on their mission. I reached out to my viewing audience on social media to ask for donations and toiletries. They need toiletries and food the most. It was cold out there for the people. People started responding through our social media sites.

We did a jacket drive at TCs Rib Crib in Las Vegas that was very successful. So many people responded to that drive in support of us. The jackets and clothes and toiletries would be useful to the people under the grounds. Although we were in our own position, I now understood why I had to take this path of homelessness. Now I had compassion for the people that we helped. I wasn't just helping them I also knew what it was like to be hungry, and go through changes with the system in Las Vegas. The city had limited resources for people in that

position. The city was now taking notice of our documentaries and effort in the community. Holy Smoke Misfit Missionaries added me to their board of directors. I was so honored to become an active board member of their nonprofit. Also, my friend Dj Thump was a popular Dj on radio station Power 88. He created what's called "The Community Spotlight." which was created to honor those that worked in the community. I was the first to receive this honor for me and my husband's work in the community. I couldn't believe that I was chosen for such an honor. We continued our work in the community, eventually starting what's called" Operation Bring Your Best." Me and my husband's service at Molasky Park turned into our direct mission. The host of volunteers was growing so fast. They kept volunteering over and over with us. I was so grateful to the volunteers that helped us serve. Some of my favorites were Melissa Howlett, John Escareno, Trese Nicole, Jenni-

fer Rowland, and Andrew Bennett just to name a few. Andrew Bennett never missed the First Sunday no matter what. He just exuded love and care with his hands-on style with the people. He always prepared soups and stews from his kitchen that fed the people. We experienced something so amazing out there that only we understood. The love for the people was our mission. All of the volunteers reached out to their people to assist us with this base. It grew so fast and helped so many people. There was a fine line between bringing cameras in and exposing the people that were in that position, but I felt as if without the awareness they wouldn't get help. I wanted to show the audience that we were really out helping the people. When Eddie put together documentaries of our work out there, it helped to spread the word about what was needed for the people. During our mission and service, I met another beautiful couple named Vaneta and Billy Easter of " ASSISTANCE OF SOUTHERN NEVADA." They were a powerful company that serviced homeless veterans. Their work in the community was amazing. When we linked with the Easters it took our mission to the next level. What I love is that they allowed us to work directly with their company showing us the executive side of running a vital Nonprofit organization. They really taught us how to use the resources to create accounts and bases that we would serve regularly. It put us in direct connection with the community. They had a donut and bread account that served the people. My husband Eddie Bell was put in charge of handling that department. Those accounts blessed so many people. People that were homeless, and those that were in need. We discovered that there were not only homeless people but also families in need that were barely getting by. Sometimes the kids were starving. The bread and donuts sometimes were the only thing that kept people going. Everyone loved to see us coming. The Easters ended up placing me on their board as well. I was now on the board for Holy Smoke Misfit Missionaries and Assistance of Southern Nevada. It was still challenging to maintain our life and put the work in, but we did what we had to do. I didn't know that our personal situation was going to turn into a passion and serve so many people. During this time we met a gentleman named Keneth Dorsey and His wife Melody Dorsey of " Planet Mike Earth. " Their Nonprofit organization serviced the youth in the community. They assisted so many families and children with resources. We also supported their movement and they came out to support Operation Bring Your Best. We were meeting so many amazing people while on this mission. Kenneth Dorsey introduced us to Justin Roberts of "True Family Services." Which was a family-run organization that serviced the community through mental health services, food resources, rental assistance for families, job resources, etc? This program was amazing. We went to interview the entire staff and some of the people that utilized their program for years. Eddie created a documentary with the interviews. Everything was in an upward motion with all of the programs that we worked with. It was so powerful to be in our position but yet God was using our life to impact so

many lives. The highlight for me was when Minister Stretch Sanders honored me at an event called " A Gathering for Black Women," with a Sister of The Year Award. Omg, I was so shocked because I didn't see this one coming. Our work was also highlighted in UK Based Magazine Soul Central and On The Rise Magazine. Through all of our ups and downs, God Knew that we had to go through being homeless to understand how much greater we would be of service to others.

Chapter 6
Create A Lane

Homelessness is a very difficult position to be in. One day we had to transition between weekly and had to rent a U-Haul truck to transport our items. We had no car at the time so this Uhaul became our vehicle for a couple of days. It's way more expensive because the u-haul is calculating per mile, but we had to do what we had to do. During that transition of having this u-haul, I had to do hair. The Uhaul is how I made it to my client. After getting done with hair, we went around town running errands and taking care of a few things so that we can post up. The weekly wasn't going to be ready until 8 am the next morning at Siegal Suites. We had nowhere to go so we hung out in the Uhaul. Well, nightfall came around and we prepared our children that we all had to sleep in the U Haul that night. Of course, the kids asked us "Why?" I had to explain to them that we were going to be in another hotel first thing in the morning. There was only real space for 2 adults in the front part of the U-haul, but we had to Squeeze six bodies in that small space. There were bodies piled upon each other. Luckily the kid's bodies were still small. I held one twin, Eddie held the other and the other two were in the middle. I couldn't sleep that good because of where we were parked. We were parked in some random parking lot at an apartment complex. My husband eventually got out of the car and stood guard over us. I woke up and asked him, "Are you ok out there?" Yes, I'm good, just making sure no one rolls upon us." This drew tears to my eyes because he was actually standing guard of his family. He made sure that no one touched us while we were sleeping. He got back in the truck and we all finally fell into a deep sleep, which is hard while you're sitting straight up. At about 4:15 A.M. we get a knock on the window with a cop's baton. "Please raise down the window slowly." "Ok officer, what's the problem?" "One of the residents here called us because this truck appeared suspicious." We explained, " We're trying to wait until the morning so that we can check into Siegal Suites. We only have a couple of hours before it opens." "Give me your I.d.s please." "No problem." They came back up to the truck and gave us our I.D. back and said, " Were going to let you

go, just make sure that you check into the weekly. We just had to come out and do a wellness check, because someone called. You guys have a good night." I was so annoyed that someone was butting in our business and we almost got us arrested. We checked into the weekly the next morning, and everything went smoothly. It was something about this location that had our creative juices flowing. I would lay down to sleep at night and would be awakened with stories. At first, I thought it was the fact that I was in a strange place, but I started writing my ideas down. Those long nights of not being able to sleep turned into a script. This script was about my homeless experience called "Walking By Faith." How is that you're still in the middle of being in the position but yet, this type of phenomenon is happening I was so spiritually awake. Not only did I write the script, but I also started formulating who the cast would be in my mind. I had a history of casting and knew exactly who I wanted for the role of Me and Eddie. There was an up and coming strong actress named Tameika Thomas who would be perfect to play the role of Queen g and a gentleman by the name of Keithen Polk who would be perfect to play the role of Eddie.

These two together would be able to pull it off. I finished the script within 30 days and immediately approached the two of them to see if they would be interested in the roles. When they both accepted we started thinking about who we would choose to play our kids and the foster family that took us in. I found people for all of these roles. My foster couple was a beautiful couple named Kathy and Conrad Dematties who lived in Delaware. I know I was reaching when I chose them, because they were a white couple which was not the original race of the couple in our real-life story, and they lived out of state. This couple had love between each other and a very strong audition, and that's the dynamic that I needed for the roles of the foster couple. I could feel the roles come alive when they submitted their audition reel. We had our main cast and the rest would be filled in roles. I registered the script, then set up

a cast meeting with the cast that was selected. I explained to this cast that this piece was about our homeless experience and that what we are currently going through it now. When we revealed to them that we were still homeless they couldn't believe it and they grew even more interested in the project. I was especially excited about the couple that we chose. We had everyone sign confidentiality forms and scheduled our first shoot on the night of my real birthday bash at a karaoke hat party. We wanted to use the crowd and the people to be apart of the scene. We had the honor and pleasure of casting Melvin Jackson Jr. best known for his role in the New Edition Film as Curtis Blow. My God I knew that this film was going to be a masterpiece. The first shooting night went well, and we partied and danced for the rest of the night away. I had close to 200 guests that evening, so it was definitely a fun birthday bash. While working on our film, I submitted for a film and play called "Is That Man Your Husband Or Is He Mine." cast and written by Ms.Michelle Boykin creator of The LasVegas Black Film festival. I auditioned and landed the role. All the while I'm saying to myself, "How am I going to take this role on while having an active talk show "Morning tea with the Queens." and work on a script and play all at the same time?" As I ask that question to myself I had to also answer it with "You can do anything that you put your mind to. "The rehearsals got underway for the play and film and I was scared out of my mind. I was afraid because I worked in casting but never had a major role. I got into rehearsals and my real life was hard. I didn't have a lot of money, hardly any food, and sometimes didn't even have a way to rehearsal. I had to reach somewhere deep to do this. I started learning lines and rehearsing with the cast and literally had to remove myself from what was going on at home. Sometimes I was sad, and it took everything in me not to break down and cry. I used my sorrow to place it into my role. My character was a church mother who had to twerk, turn up, cry, and she was a hot mess. I would put everything into the character and leave home at home. As we got closer to showtime on the movie rehearsals increased and we also started scheduling dates to shoot the film. It was time for me to have a candid conversation with the director. One evening I asked her to take me home because I didn't have a ride and she told me that she would take me. During that ride home I opened up and told her the truth." Ms. Michelle, I just wanted to let you know I'm homeless." I'm only revealing this due to the fact that coming to all of the rehearsals may be a little challenge." She said, " I don't know why you didn't tell me sooner." " I didn't tell you before now because I wanted to prove to you that I really wanted this role and that I was trying. Now that I haven't missed a rehearsal, I thought it was time to reveal the news. " Well, it' s ok a closed mouth doesn't get fed, and don't worry about nothing I will personally make sure that you get to and from rehearsals even if I have to take you myself." "Well thank you. "Getting this news off of my chest was a big relief. Now she knew if I didn't necessarily make it to all of the rehearsals that it was a real reason, not because I'm just taking the day off. Rehearsals increased for the play while also filming the movie. It was my test to see what I was made of. I was stressed more than ever because I really didn't know how we were going to keep this roof over our heads, but God had us the whole time. Some donations started pouring in from our efforts in the community, so the donations helped and I had some generous friends that sent me money over and over again, and that helped us to pay our rent weekly. Sometimes food was scarce, but we did what we had to do. It was time to get on stage for the play, and I was nervous but also anticipating the play wrapping so that I could focus on my family. I had so much support shockingly that came from near and far to see me in the play. The support fired me up. We had three amazing shows and just like that it was over. I felt like I was out of my body. I felt so accomplished and the tears that I shed on stage as one of the mothers of the church were real tears so I wasn't acting. The feedback from people was amazing. They told me that when I cried on stage, it made them cry. They felt all of the emotion from the role. I am so grateful that I accomplished so much while being in a space where I lost it all. As soon as the film and play wrapped, we started filming our movie. The filming process was difficult because the scenes were my life. Sometimes I was so emotional that the cast had to hold me in between scenes. The most emotional scene is when The foster family had to tell us that we had to leave their homes. These actors were so authentic that it felt real and they had to hold me during filming. I learned so much about myself during this time. Me and my husband did a lot of praying and holding each other up in support. I believe it was through the creative process of these projects that helped us to make me through our homeless moment. We had a focus and something to keep our attention on while being down. People don't realize how creative arts actually save people's lives. It saved our life.

Chapter 7
I'm Finally Home

I received a call from my daughter Star Rolle One day, she said " Mom, I'm going to help you get an apartment." "What you mean?" "I have A1 credit, and I'm going to apply for an apartment for you, you just would have to come up with the move-in costs, and keep up the rent and the utilities." "Well after being out here on the streets with the kids for a whole year and a half, that wouldn't be an issue. I don't care what it takes, I just need to be settled again." She stated, " Mom let me call you back, I'm going to make a few calls, and If I can get you to be the one to do all of the transactions we'll be in business." She made a few calls, and the next thing that I knew, I got a call back from her saying that we have a lead. She gave me the address to the property, told me to take a 40 money order there for the rental credit check, and that's what I did. I met with the apartment complex manager, and she took me into the upstairs 2 bedroom 2 bath fully loaded condo unit to supposedly take pics and do a video for Star, but it was really for us. The condo was beautiful and also very spacious. I crossed my fingers that everything would go through ok. I spent the next couple of days on pins and needles. The manager spoke as if it was already ours, and I lined my faith up with the way that she spoke. When I left to head back to the hotel heading toward the bus stop, I prayed over that entire block and claimed it as our new street. The street was called Simmons Street. This area was a huge step up from the hotels that we had been living in, and it had better quality schools and in a neater area. My anticipation grew for what the answer would be. The next day I received a call from my friend Naomi that lives in New Mexico, and She gave me the news that she would allow me to borrow her car. She would fly in and out of Vegas all of the time and grow weary of the expenses from renting cars when she would get to Vegas. Her bringing her car down was a win-win for both of us and she only needed the vehicle when she would come to town which was like every other month. I told her yes I would be willing to keep her car and do pick up and drop-offs to the airport. I'm thinking that she would be bringing the car in the near future, but no God had another plan. She drove the car down the next day. I was in shock that we would go suddenly from months of being on the bus to suddenly having access to a car. God was opening doors for us that at one point seemed impossible. When she pulled up in the car I was so ecstatic. We seemed to be in a living nightmare for so long, and it was nice to get some good news for a change. I thanked my friend so many times and cried at the same time. My appointments were so much simpler. I loved the convenience of just getting up and going and not being faced with spending hours on the bus just for one appointment. Thank God something good was happening for my family. My babies were so happy too. They grew weary of walking everywhere or catching the bus.

Chapter 8
The Approval

I received the call that I was waiting for. My daughter let me know 48 hours after applying for the condo that we were approved. The move-in costs would be just $400 due to her A1 credit. The thing is I was a bit nervous about move-in costs, but after going hungry, sleeping on people's floors, sleepless nights sleeping in the car, no stability for almost two years, we were going to find a way to come up with move-in costs by any means necessary. I started reaching out to people for help and working non-stop. We let go of our rent in the weekly too to make it happen. We figured that we could come back and square them away later. We made a quick $ho150 donating plasma. This was survival of the fittest, any mean necessary. After about four days of non-stop hustle we came up with our move in. I was so happy. After almost two years of stress, this amazing door was finally opened. The day came for me to take move-in costs, and I was so happy. We had already started breaking our weekly down. We basically gave a lot of things away. We didn't want to walk into our new place with things that we didn't need. I went and turned in the money and the manager agreed to hand over the keys. We basically told her that Star works a lot. So Star had to write to her and get permission to give me the keys. I couldn't believe this was really happening, and finally, my prayers were breaking through to God. I didn't know how we were going to maintain an $1100 rent after being homeless for almost two years, but I didn't care how we had to do it ,we had to make it happen. On move-in day, I went live on Facebook to show my viewers that God made a way for us. I received the highest amount of views that day. People had witnessed the struggle with us, so our victory was also their victory. Our prayers and their prayers had been answered. I shared my moment with the world and it felt amazing. Nothing could bring my high of life down. I just kept saying Thank you, Jesus, for keeping us.

Chapter 9
FOUR HEARTBEATS

No one suffered more than my four children while experiencing homelessness. When we were packing up our three bedroom home, they were little, but I could just see their faces. They didn"t quite understand why we had to move from our comfortable home where things were right at their fingertips, to being crammed in one room. I would have to reassure them daily that everything was going to be okay. I would tell them that, but not sure if that was true or even if the door was going to open again for us to be stable again.It mentally broke me down to see them cry, and be hungry some days. Sleeping in the car with mommy and daddy was so uncomfortable due to the fact that they were piled up on each other. They were normally able to choose where there want to be. It was a major adjustment for them altogether. I remember taking a trip from California to Vegas to make sure that they got to school. We pulled into a gas station, and I had to get into the backseat of my truck to comb their hair. That morning I had to take them into the gas station bathroom to wash their faces and dress them. In my mind i'm thinking "I have to send them school so that they can eat." We made sure that no matter what that they made it to school. In spite of our situation we wanted to make sure that they got their education. During the course of our almost two years of homelessness ,they changed schools four times. It was taking a toll on their health, self-esteem, and appearance and began to break them down mentally. I knew what I was dealing with just trying to keep a roof over their heads, but they had been ripped from everything. It's going to hit home and affect them like it did us. One time I had to go into Serenity's class and speak with her teacher.

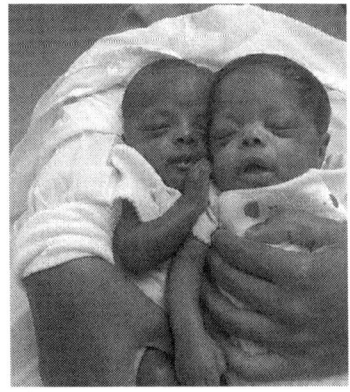

She was smart ,but they were getting ready to retain her due to failing grades and missing assignments. During that parent conference I explained our situation and let her know that before Serenity got to her she had two other teachers within a span of months. She's confused, hurting, and has been uprooted from0 ty everything that she knows. She now understood why Serenity was going through changes in class. Once we had that talk we all had to tag-team just to make sure that she passed that year. My kids also suffered from depression. They went through a lot of tears, and confusion. When we moved into the weekly that was walking distance from their school that is when things turned around for the kids. We stayed in

The Siegal Suites across from Molasky Park the longest. Due to some stability, their grades turned around and they began to excel. That 8 months that we lived in Siegal Suites, the kids started getting in those books and doing very well even getting on The honor Rolls list a couple of times. My son brought home Straight A's during that time. I was so proud of my babies especially with what we had experienced. Here I am thinking that we were failing my babies, but they were thriving on our strength, not the failure aspect. I was so amazingly happy to discover that fact and I was very proud of them. The revelation was so powerful, I went to social media and spoke about it. One main lesson that I learned going through this is that you have to keep your family together no matter what!

Chapter 10
Awareness

When our life took a twist and turn I was so angry. I was angry with life and angry at God, asking the question " How could you let this happen to us." Going through homelessness made me realize the important lesson " Trust the process." Life is full of mystery and full of things that we just don't quite understand, but through this experience, I learned so many amazing lessons. Number 1, I learned that my life does not belong to me and that I'm simply a vessel used by God to operate his powerful message through. Suffering sometimes turns into purpose. I wouldn't have ever learned that there is a hurting homeless society that people look down on every day. Homelessness can affect every race and every walk of life. Every person that lives on the street, and that's dirty doesn't make them mentally unstable. It is a good reason as to why they got there. This experience drew me closer to God than ever and took my spiritual awareness to another level. Now I understood why I had to lose it all. God was trying to birth things though me but couldn't due to the fact that I was distracted with life. When It was taken, and when I was tested, I was now forced to listen to God and follow the instructions of the voice that I was hearing, and not ignore it anymore. Scripts, movies, books, and homeless programs were birthed from this time in my life. Although we felt as if God abandoned us, he never left us and was carrying the whole time. I can now honestly say that I'm happy that our life took this course and that it taught us how to open up and care for a society that people overlook every day. Through the trial of what we went through it built character in us and made us better people. My children are powerful and amazing to go through this with us, I love them unconditionally. Our marriage was tested, but through love and faith we stuck it out. I'm so grateful that we were able to keep our family together. GOD'S Favor was upon us!

If you look at this handsome face, you would never believe that he is homeless because of how attractive he is. I met this gentleman one night from a spontaneous idea to go out to Molasky Park and give out jackets to those that were in the winter weather. I learned the lesson that you can't judge a book by its cover, and that homelessness can touch the lives of people from different walks of life. The gentleman thanked me and I went to the next person that needed a jacket. I went home that evening to look at the pics and this one stood out to me the most. When I see this photo he was very distinguished and seemed to be in his right mind. I'm sure at one point in his life he was very productive and had it all, but lost it for whatever reason. You're looking at two faces that were affected by the homeless, so again never judge a book by its cover.

COMMUNITY REPORT

Queen G. and a host of friends and family got together on September 2nd, 2018 to feed and clothe the homeless at Molasky Park in Las Vegas Nevada. The mission is called "Operation# Bring Your Best". This mission was created by Shonta Gibson after losing her home, cars, etc. due to her husband's health condition after suffering a stroke. After losing it all, they stayed with different people and is weekly's to try to keep a roof over their head. While trying to recover both health wise and personally they met Emma Mcclenaghan and Arthur Mcclean of Organization "Holy Smoke MoOr Missionaries," which goes into the tunnels of Las Vegas to feed the homeless. Joining forces and creating a documentary about the life of The homeless living under the grounds of Las Vegas. With this new awareness of the extensive homeless issue in Las Vegas, "Operation# Bring Your Best," was created to feed and clothe the homeless. This mission meets every first Sunday at Molasky park. The goal is to bring more heightened awareness to the homeless problem in Las Vegas and ultimately getting people off the streets and back into a thriving society.

This raised awareness in Las Vagas of the Homeless Community Social Media Exposer with the Community Report with Queen G. Magazine Article

Community Resources: Las Vegas

All Shades United
Minister Stretch
702 809-4599

Better Minds Bettet Communities
702 695-5643

True Family Services
702 463-0110

Mass Liberation
323 926-6998

Progressive Leadership Alliance of Nevada
702 292-1279

Las Vegas Black Pschology Association
702 825-0828

We Shine Studios
702 202-7903

Sistas That Paint
559 974-2607

Education for Quality Living
702 612-5838

Grace Immanuel Missionary Baptist Church
702 378-0770

SNS Events
702 308-3262

Planned Parenthood
775 781-4649

Catholic Charities of Southern Nevada
702 385-2662

Catholic Charities Shelter for Men Las Vegas
702 387-2282

Las Vegas Rescue Mission
702 382-1766

Nevada South Search and Rescue
702 850-0512

Planet Mike Earth Youth Organization
Keneth Dorsey Melody Dorsey
702 741-5719
909 693-0542

The Shade Tree
For Homeless and Abused Women
702 385-0072

Community Health Charities
702 433-6709

Southern Nevada Children First
702 487-5665

Family Promise of Las Vegas
702 638-8806

Salvation Army Path
702 701-5368

Safe Nest For Women
702 646-4981

Nevada Partnership For Homeless Youth
702 383-1332

Womens Development Center
702 796-7770

Assistance of Southern Nevada
For Homeless Veterans
Billy Easter 702 479-8447

Follow me on Social Media to see and hear more Amazing Things!

@queengliveexperience

LGEN Films

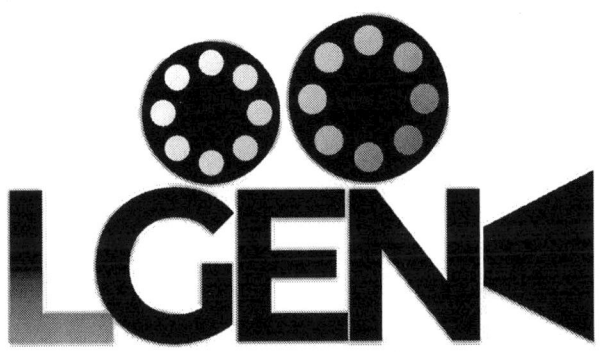

BOOK TODAY!

- Media
- Marketing
- Red Carpet Events
- Promo Vedios
- Networking
- Music Vedios
- Photo Shoots

LGEN2018AUG@GMAIL.COM

Graphic design and formating by:
Go-Getta-DaPaper-Boi
Marissa Mange with Blue Flame Graphics

"The Message You Portray Is The Design We Convey"

 Blue Flame Graphics   @ blueflame_graphics